PIANO · VOCAL · GUITAR

ISBN 1-4234-0900-0

HAL•LEONARD®
CORPORATION
7777 W. BLUEMOUND RD. P.O. BOX 13819 MILWAUKEE, WI 53213

Visit Hal Leonard Online at
www.halleonard.com

CONTENTS

STAND UP FOR LOVE

Words and Music by DAVID FOSTER
and AMY FOSTER-GILLIES

INDEPENDENT WOMEN PART I

Words and Music by CORY ROONEY,
SAMUEL BARNES, JEAN CLAUDE OLIVIER
and BEYONCÉ KNOWLES

Lyrics (from the vocal line):

Spoken: Lu-cy Liu with my girl Drew Cam'ron D.___ and Des-ti-ny, Char-lie's An-gels come on.

Sung: Ques-tion: Tell me what you think a-bout __ me.__ I buy my own dia-monds and I buy my own __ rings.__ On-ly ring your

SURVIVOR

Words and Music by BEYONCÉ KNOWLES,
ANTHONY DENT and MATTHEW KNOWLES

Recorded a half step lower.

SOLDIER

Words and Music by BEYONCÉ KNOWLES,
KELLY ROWLAND, SEAN GARRETT,
RICH HARRISON, MICHELLE WILLIAMS,
DWAYNE CARTER and CLIFFORD HARRIS

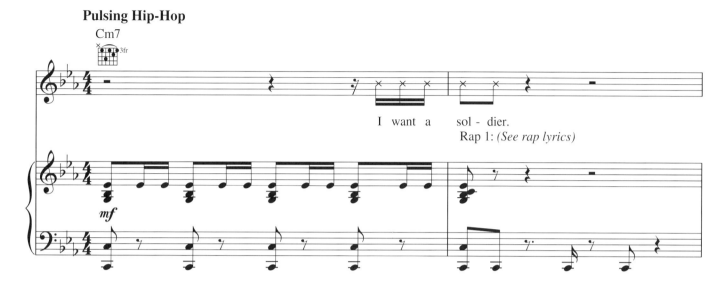

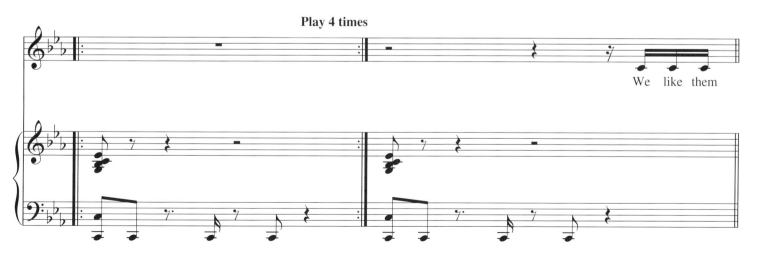

stat - us ain't hood, I ain't check - in' for him.

Bet - ter be street if he look - in' at me.____ I need a

sol - dier that ain't scared to stand up for me.____ Got - ta

know to get dough,__ and he bet - ter be street.__ We like them

put - tin' that on me. (Where they at?) Rap 2: *(See rap lyrics)*

If your stat - us ain't hood, I ain't check - in' for him.

Bet - ter be street if he look - in' at me.____ I need a

sol - dier that ain't scared to stand up for me,____ known to

car - ry big things,___ if you know what I mean.___ If your

stat - us ain't hood, (ain't hood,) I ain't check - in' for him.

Bet - ter be street if he look - in' at me.___ I need a

To Coda ⊕

sol - dier that ain't scared to stand up for me.___ Got - ta

D.S. al Coda

CODA

"That one may be the one to-night."___ If your know to get dough,___ and he bet-ter be street.___ I know some sol-diers in here. (Where they at? Where they at?) They wan-na take care of me. (Where they at?) I know some

sol - diers in here. (Where they at? Where they at?) Would - n't mind

put - tin' that on me. (Where they at?)

Repeat and Fade | **Optional Ending**

Rap Lyrics

Rap 1: Hey, the way you got it, I'm the hottest around.
They'll know it when they see you rollin' impalas around.
With the top down, feelin' the sounds.
Quakin' and vibratin' your thighs, ridin' harder than guys.
With the chrome wheels at the bottom, white leather inside.
When them flames be spittin' at you,
Tell 'em don't even try it.
To shoot it with 'Chelle, and kick it with Kelly, or holla at B.
You gotta be g's. You way out of your league, please.

Rap 2: Hey, see, cash money is an army.
I'm walkin' with purple hearts on me.
You talkin' to the sargeant.
Body marked up like the subway in Harlem.
Call him, weezy f baby, please say the baby.
If you don't see me on the block, I ain't tryin' to hide.
I blend in with the hood, I'm camouflage.
Bandana tied, so mommy, join the troop.
Now every time she hear my name, she salute.

CHECK ON IT

Words and Music by BEYONCÉ KNOWLES,
SEAN GARRETT, SWIZZ BEATZ,
ANGELA BEYINCE and STAYVE THOMAS

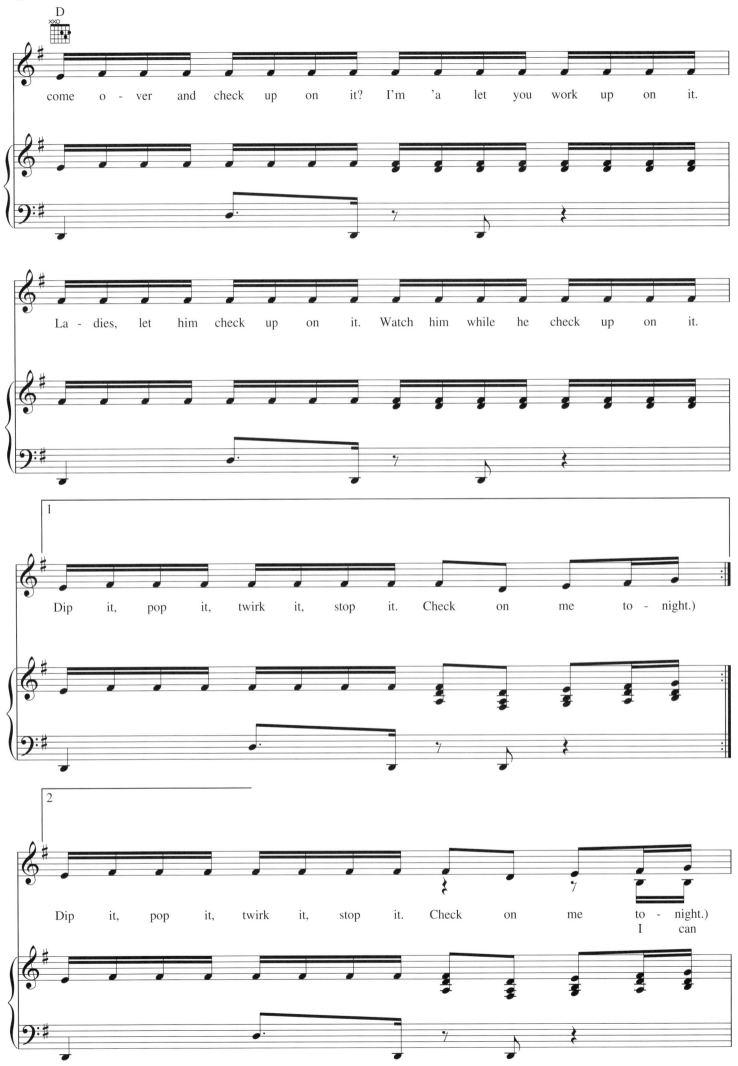

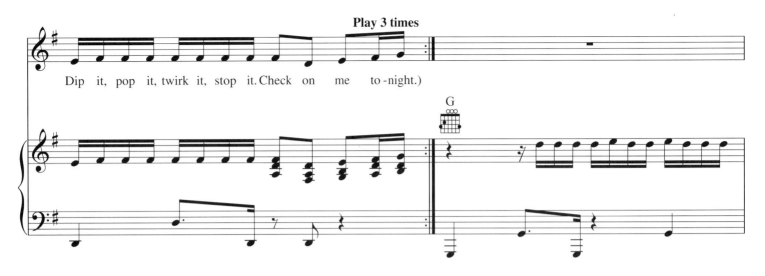

Dip it, pop it, twirk it, stop it. Check on me to-night.)

Rap Lyrics

Rap 1: You need to
Stop playin' around with all the clowns and the wangstas.
Good girls gotta get down with the gangsters.
Go 'head, girl, put some back and some neck up on it
While I stand up in the background and check up on it.

Rap 2: I'm checkin' on you, Boo; do what you do.
And while you dance I'm 'a glance at this beautiful view.
Keep my hands in my pants, I need to glue 'em with glue.
I'm in a trance, all eyes on you and your crew.
Me and my mans don't dance but can feel y'all bump and grind.
It won't hurt if you gon' try one time.
They all hot, but let me see, this one's mine.
It's Slim Thugga and D.C. outa H-Town.

JUMPIN, JUMPIN

Words and Music by BEYONCÉ KNOWLES,
RUFUS MOORE, CHAD ELLIOTT
and JOVONN ALEXANDER

Moderately

* Vocals sung an octave lower.

48

* Lead vocal part sung second time only.

*Lead vocal part sung both times.

LOSE MY BREATH

Words and Music by BEYONCÉ KNOWLES,
KELLY ROWLAND, RODNEY JERKINS,
LaSHAWN DANIELS, SHAWN CARTER,
FRED JERKINS, SEAN GARRETT
and MICHELLE WILLIAMS

Bright Dance beat

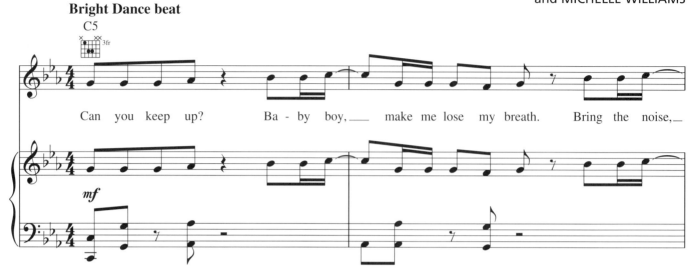

Can you keep up? Ba - by boy,___ make me lose my breath. Bring the noise,___

___ make me lose my breath. Hit me hard,___ make me lose my. (Hah. Hah.)

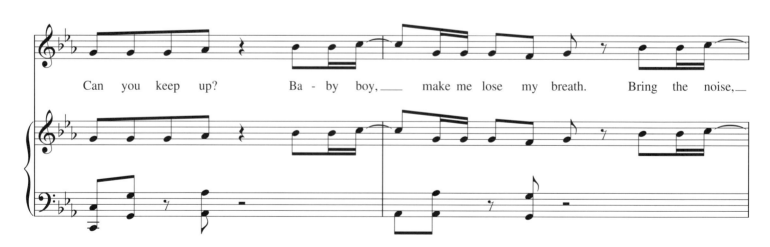

Can you keep up? Ba - by boy,___ make me lose my breath. Bring the noise,___

60

make me lose my breath. Hit me hard, ___ make me lose my breath.

Ooh, two things I don't like when I'm try-in' to get my
Ooh, you un-der-stand the facts that I'm try-in' to give to

groove, is a part-ner that meets me on-ly half-way, and just can't
you? You __ mov-in' so slow like you just don't have a

prove. _____ Take me out so deep when you know you can't swim.
clue. _____ Did-n't ma-ma teach you to give af-fec - tion? You're the

can't make me say "Ooh,"_____ like the beat of this groove,_____

you don't have no busi - ness in this. Here's your pa - pers, ba - by, you are dis - missed.

(Dis - missed, dis - missed, dis - missed, dis - missed, dis - missed, dis - missed, dis - missed, dis - missed.)

D.S. al Coda
(with repeat)

CODA

Repeat and Fade

make me lose my breath.

Optional Ending

SAY MY NAME

Words and Music by RODNEY JERKINS,
LaSHAWN DANIELS, FRED JERKINS,
BEYONCÉ KNOWLES, KELENDRIA ROWLAND,
LaTAVIA ROBERSON and LeTOYA LUCKETT

EMOTION

Words and Music by BARRY GIBB
and ROBIN GIBB

A - yeah, A - yeah. yeah, yeah, Ooh, yeah.

2. *(Lead vocal ad lib.)*

It's o-ver and done, ___ but the heart-ache lives on ___ in-side
there at your side, ___ a ___ part of all the_ things you are.

(Yeah, yeah.)

and who is the one you're cling - ing _ to ___
But you've got a part of some - one _ else.

BUG A BOO

Words and Music by KANDI L. BURRUSS,
KEVIN BRIGGS, BEYONCÉ KNOWLES, KELENDRIA ROWLAND,
LaTAVIA ROBERSON and LeTOYA LUCKETT

Steadily, half-time feel

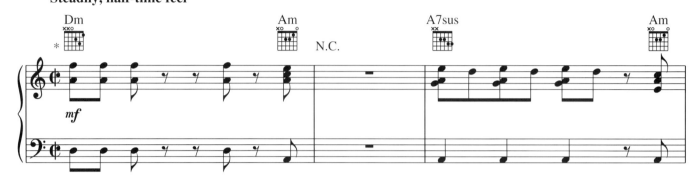

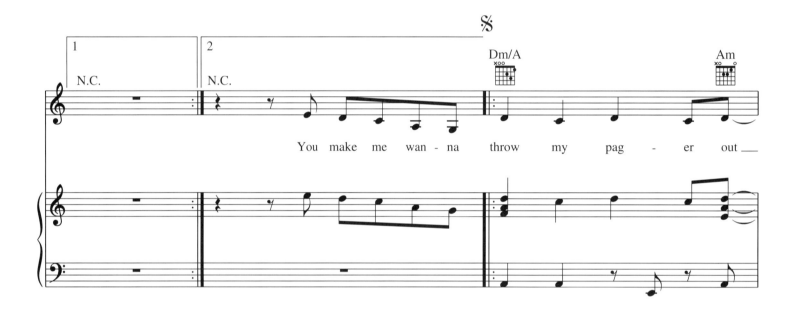

You make me wan-na throw my pag-er out ___

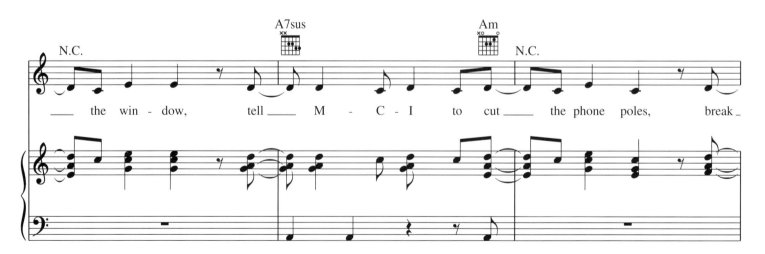

___ the win-dow, tell ___ M - C - I to cut ___ the phone poles, break ___

* Recorded a half step lower.

BOOTYLICIOUS

Words and Music by BEYONCÉ KNOWLES,
ROB FUSARI, FALONTE MOORE
and STEVIE NICKS

Medium Hip-Hop

Kel - ly can you han - dle this? Mich - elle, can you han - dle this? Be -

yon - cé, can you han - dle this? I don't think they can han - dle this.

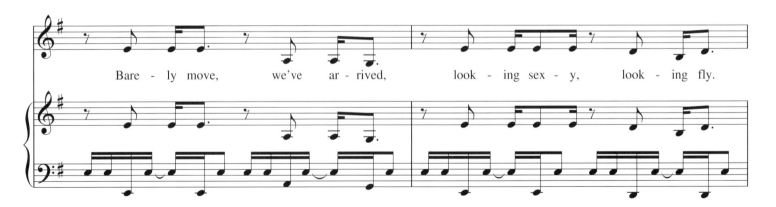

Bare - ly move, we've ar - rived, look - ing sex - y, look - ing fly.

* *Recorded a half step lower.*

Ba - by, can you han - dle this? I don't think you can han - dle this.

I'm a - bout to break you off, H - town___ go - ing hard.

Lead my hips, slap my thighs, swing my hair, square my eyes.

Look - ing hot, smell - ing good, groov - ing like___ I'm from the hood.

BILLS, BILLS, BILLS

Words and Music by KANDI L. BURRUSS,
KEVIN BRIGGS, BEYONCÉ KNOWLES,
KELENDRIA ROWLAND and LeTOYA LUCKETT

At first we start-ed out real cool,
Now you've been max-in' out my card,

tak-in' me plac-es I had nev-er ___ been. ___ But now ___
gave me bad cred-it, buy me gifts with ___ my ___ own name. ___

GIRL

Words and Music by BEYONCÉ KNOWLES,
KELLY ROWLAND, EDDIE ROBINSON, DON DAVIS,
ANGELA BEYINCE, SEAN GARRETT, MICHELLE WILLIAMS
and PATRICK DOUTHIT

Take a min-ute, girl,___ come sit down,___ and
See, what y'all___ don't know a-bout him,___ is I

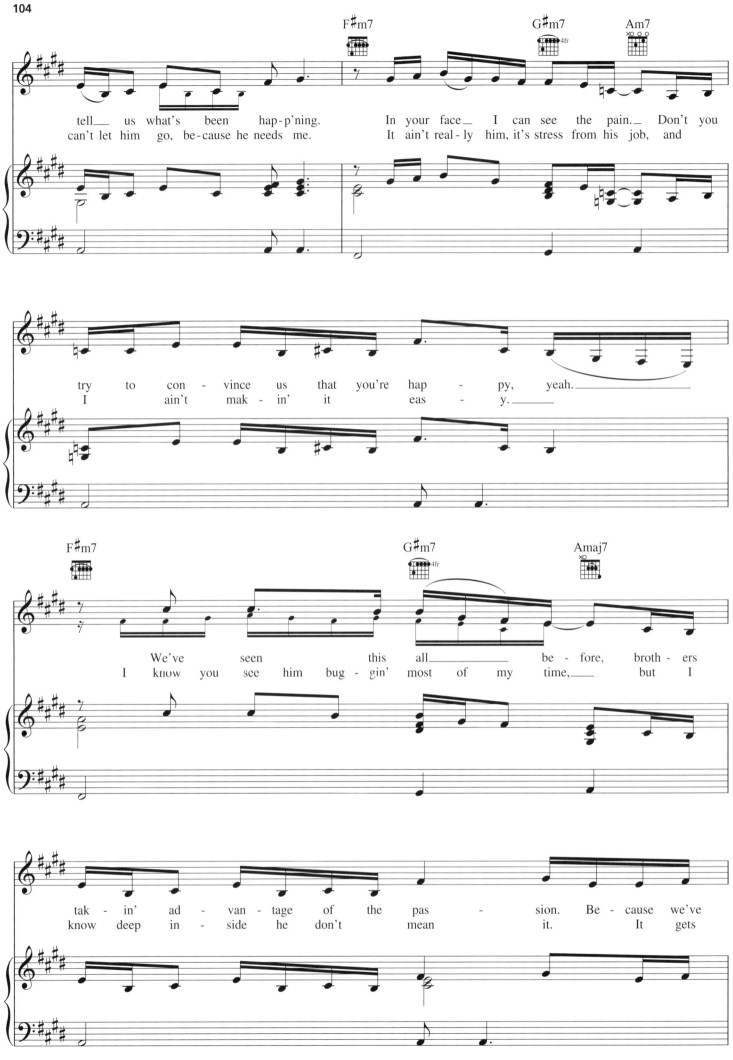

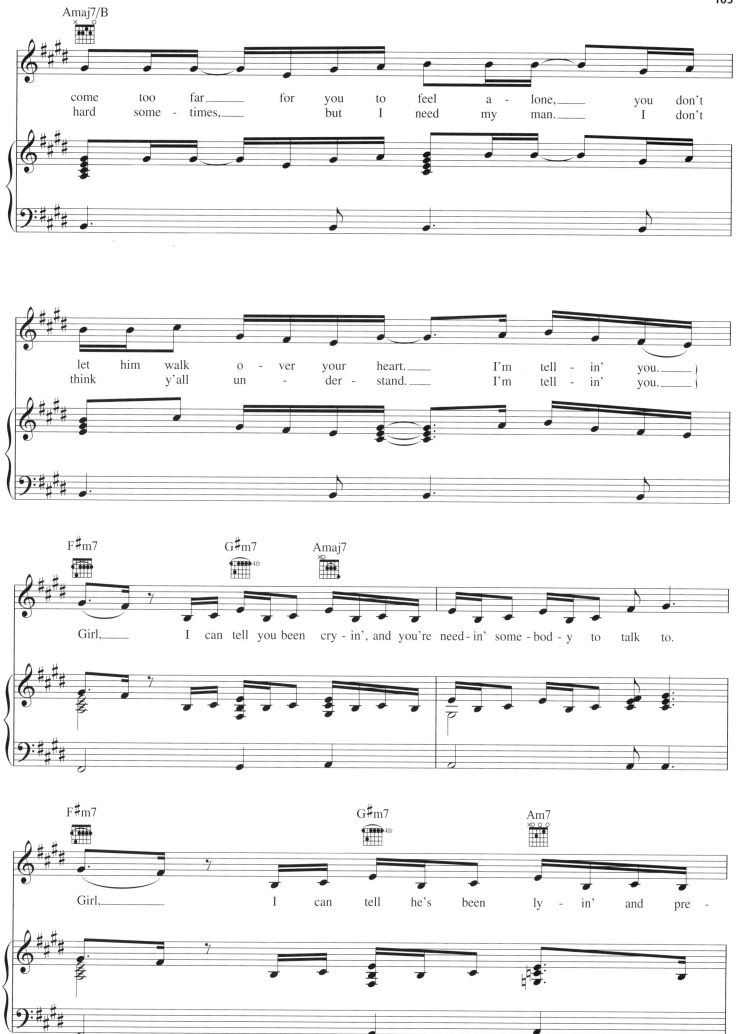

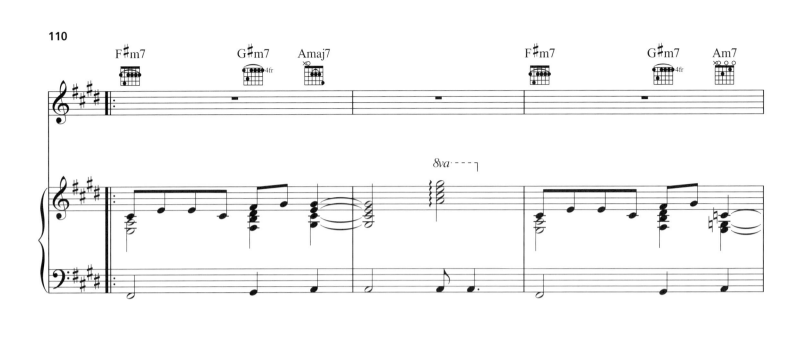

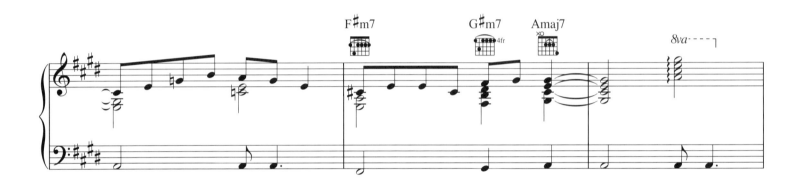

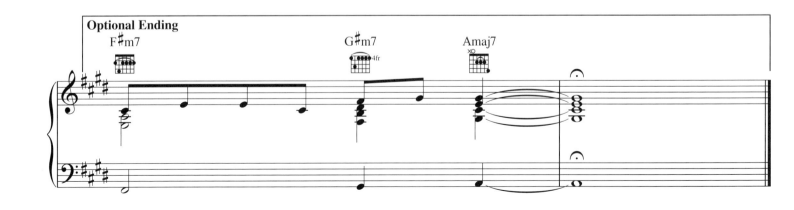

NO, NO, NO PART 2

Words by BARRY WHITE, MARY BROWN,
CALVIN C. GAINES and VINCENT J. HERBERT
Music by BARRY WHITE, ROBERT FUSARI
and VINCENT J. HERBERT

Rap Lyrics

Yo, close your eyes, shorty. You're guaranteed to be hypnotized
By the remix that Wyclef provide. I don't
Care about your size. Girl, shake your thighs. All I'm
Trying to do in the hood is stay alive,
Make a little money with Destiny's Child.
Thugs hear this song, they dance, they go wild like
Texas. They moving like no-limit soldiers. They
Went from a dream to the young Supremes. Sing it.

CATER 2 U

Words and Music by BEYONCÉ KNOWLES,
KELLY ROWLAND, RODNEY JERKINS,
ROBERT WALLER, RIC RUDE
and MICHELLE WILLIAMS

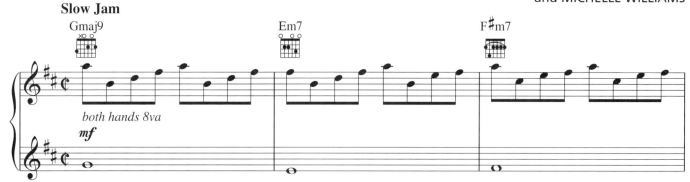

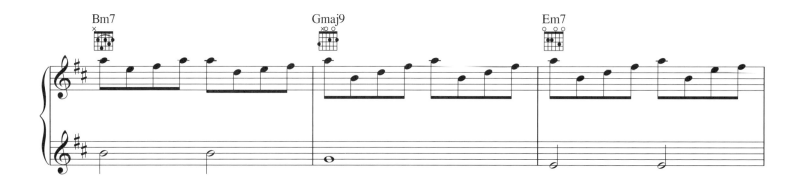

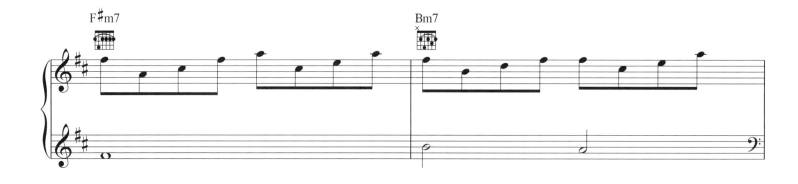

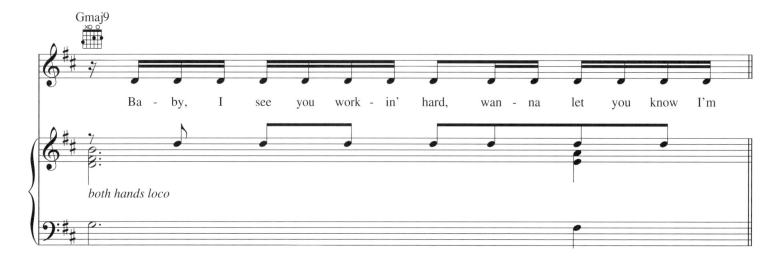

Ba - by, I see you work - in' hard, wan - na let you know I'm

FEEL THE SAME WAY I DO

Words and Music by BEYONCÉ KNOWLES,
KELLY ROWLAND, MICHELLE WILLIAMS,
RODNEY JERKINS, LaSHAWN DANIELS,
FRED JERKINS and RICKY LEWIS